My Truth
The Birthing

Nicole Watson

Copyright © 2018 Nicole Watson

All rights reserved.

ISBN 10: 0692975438
ISBN-13: 978-0692975435

DEDICATION

This book is dedicated to those experiencing the birthing pains during your journey of becoming. May this book bring clarity, direction, and transparency loud and clear. Healing is your portion. Open your heart and receive. Now is your time.

My Truth The Birthing

FOREWORD BY ZONYA MARAET

Finesse the process. From beginning to end, we journey alongside the author through pain, birth, death, rebirth, and evolution. With the turn of every page, you will revel in emotion and encounter the climax of a faith filled montage through an eclipsed vision only to be immersed into the abyss of divine shifting. Ordered steps begin to manifest through supernatural uprising causing a catalyst of light in the most intimate intricacies of the heart. Matters of the mind become shadows of tainted dreams depleted by overdrawn banks of inflated Godly purpose. A paradigm shift will derail meager personal gains for destined alignment. This is what "My Truth-The Birthing" unveils to its readers. You are invited to sail the sea of life tethered to the waves of the Kings glory boisterously chanting His spoken Word over her life. Chains? Broken. Fear? Diminished. Strongholds? Dismantled. Enemy? Defeated. Life? Restored. Joy? Fulfilled. Confidence? Renewed. Purpose? Birthed. Step by step, measure by measure, faith to faith, and glory to glory; the anomaly of rebirth will begin to orchestrate the anatomy of your spirit. Surmounted by blessed hope, you will also climb the mountain of tribulation in order to withstand the wiles of self-induced proclivities in exchange for the beauty of things not seen. "My Truth-The Birthing" will fertilize your seed of truth and produce a lifelong cycle of new birth. It is the essence of transformation documenting the photosynthesized passage from cocoon to butterfly.

FOREWORD BY DANIEL HARRIS

This book is undoubtedly a must read. Each line is more than an average storyline, it is a divine download perfectly crafted with the intent to create a paradigm shift for each reader. Nicole's eclectic writing style is both prolific and prophetic. Prepare your hearts and minds to embrace a perspective of life that is the pulse, heartbeat and revelations of Nicole Watson.

My Truth The Birthing

CONTENTS

The Process

Stages

Searching

Fear

Safety

Shoes Untied

Power

Hunger

Courage

Dust Settles

LEGGO Joy

My Declaration

His Royal Majesty

Fight

Triumph

Foot Movement

Rain

My Truth The Birthing

He Wins, I Win

A New Woman

True Inner Beauty

A Beautiful Flower

Harvest

Gloves Handed Over

A Deeper Wound

A Different Wound

Motherhood

Surrender

My Love For Him

Love Letter

Strength

Little Black Girl

Encouragement

Ride Or Die

Strength

Growth

Change

Wed

Moving On

The Journey Continues

My Truth The Birthing

THE PROCESS

For years I've imagined
Dreaming of the day that everything would be just ok
A day when I would finally be able to breathe beyond worry and discouragement
I wondered
When I would finally see what you see
Inside of myself
My life
And my spirit
I wanted to have eyes to see
Ears to hear
And the mind of the king but later I discovered
I already carry what I needed

At twenty-eight years old my eyes opened
My ears popped
And my mind and focus shifted
Just enough
So I could tap into this thing called life
Meaning I had the opportunity to live
Something I never really did
For me
For years I poured my life into my loved ones
My friends
And family to the point I forgot about me
I counseled and listened to everyone else's problems and issues and carried their burdens in my heart
When really I needed a listening ear
I never had the opportunity to discover myself
What I liked

My Truth The Birthing

What I wanted in life

The real me
And not what people wanted me to be
I thought it was too late at this point
Liker there weren't many opportunities left
Thinking here I am almost thirty years old
Fearful
Not where I know I want to be
And my time is gone

Isn't that something
I never had the chance to really live
And pursue my passions

In reality
I thought I was confident
I lived as a little girl in fear
I thought I was outspoken
I was quiet
I thought I was full of courage
I was full of fear
I thought I trusted you
I worried
Now
Here I am
In this thing called the process
Writing poems
Through moments of transparency
To reach listening ears and open hearts

It begins
Enter
My Truth
The Birthing

My Truth The Birthing

STAGES

Everyone experiences seasons in life that mods, shapes, and transforms us. It is up to us if we grow or repeat those seasons that ultimately become cycles.

SEARCHING

I'm soul searching
For a place that brings me comfort
Makes me feel at home
Like a newborn baby
Waiting to be swept into its mother's arms
Searching
For a chance to be loved
By something or someone
Whether it's a puppy at a store
Or a little child that runs to me lost
Trying to find its way home
Searching
For an answer
That will soon pass my way
As I catch its truthfulness
Many people run from reality because they lack spiritual mindedness
Like knowing that god is the only way to truthfully turn to
Besides his son Jesus
Searching
For a new walk
A new talk
A new sense of personality
Instead of being dragged into an uncomfortable sense of self-worth given to me by a world lacking self-expression
Searching
For that cloud of sunshine that will one day overtake the darkness

My Truth The Birthing

And become
An undeniable love built upon realizing its reality
I am truly searching
For life's breath
And fresh air that brings my thoughts to a waterfall
With never-ending motions, love, natural healings, peace, flowing rivers of long lost hopes and dreams
Filled with so much love
A little child would never want to leave because it feels secure
I
Am
Searching
For my future of everlasting remembrance
Just by living
A life
Without stress
Searching
For Mr. right
But who am I kidding
No one is perfect
But I still want real love
I
Am
Searching
Am I selfish?
For wanting and searching for a life with God and all that I desire?
He always told me to ask and I shall receive
On that note
I will continue to search for happiness, never ending stories, peace and gratefulness

So excuse me
My journey
Is starting

My Truth The Birthing

FEAR

Astronauts overcome insecurity of failing the mission
First time mothers overcome fears of labor
Sky divers move amongst the wind
Beyond intimidation of height and speed
Every day someone is fighting and moving past doubt
By taking their foot and moving FORWARD

SAFETY

Guard your heart.

My Truth The Birthing

SHOES UNTIED

Row, row, row your boat
Gently down the stream
Merrily, merrily, merrily
Life is but a dream

Indeed

Eight years of my life flew by and I didn't get to enjoy it
I was blinded
By the fears and disappointments of my past

Let me start here

POWER

In war
There are limited rules
When overcoming
One must remember their name, destiny, and purpose
The might one gives a helping hand
Since no one can beat him
He stands to the very end

My Truth The Birthing

HUNGER

Bold hunger must align with wise hunger.

COURAGE

Pain is inferior to strength
Unspoken words
Only actions
Embark the journey
Help comes
Faith arises
Eyes are opened
Vision is clear
Forward movement unlike any time before

My Truth The Birthing

DUST SETTLES

Great vision and past behind
Depression can no longer run my life
I overcame the day I realized I was washed in the word
And the blood of Jesus impacted and lead every moment of my life
Today
I'm better
Victory
Joy
Peace
Strength
I reign daily

LEGGO JOY

Unspeakable joy
Sounds easier than done but it takes effort and the choice
to live in joy.

My Truth The Birthing

MY DECLARATION

I am God's child
I am a woman on the journey of destiny
I am pure and designed for greatness
I am chosen for such a time as this
I am a key for free the broken hearts of the lonely
I am a testimony
I am a reflection of I AM
I am a melody of God's heart
I am truth and I shall speak it
I am his beloved
I am a dream waiting to be fulfilled
I am a love song
I am freedom
I am a bird soaring amongst the earth
I am the palm tree that stands tall through the heavy winds and heavy storms
I am a banner of God's love
I am a smile that stretches to each direction even when I want to frown
I am loved
I am a Proverbs 31 woman
I am free
I am the light shining darkness
I am Esther
I am the spirit of David
I am healing
I am the bride of Christ
I am who he has called me to be

I am running after his heart
I am in love with God
I am his daughter
I am forever worshipping the king
I am strong
I am seeking him
I am fighting
I am a warrior
I am Nicole

My Truth The Birthing

HIS ROYAL MAJESTY

His royal majesty is what we call him
Although back
Then they simply called him Jesus
Now I'm not trying to tell a story of history
Because truth be told there is so much proof
If you would just open your bible
God clearly painted the picture for us all to see
I'm not talking about just Adam and Eve
But he clearly shows his miraculous deeds
Listen closely
Not only did he allow peter to walk on the water
He did something even greater
He unleashed his son named Jesus through birth in this world by a woman named Mary
Pure
She was enough
To be blessed with such a son
To not only be a carpenter
But later on
Show God's love through his actions
Healing the sick
Casting out demons
And how could I forget
Giving his own life
So that we could live
What other God do you know would give up one of his most precious sons?
So all of his children could have a chance
Full of humility Jesus did it

Whipped and chained him
They did
Causing tears and blood to shed from his body
They did
But I'm glad they did
Because if God hadn't sacrificed Jesus
Where would we be?
Would we be caught up in our own sins?
Or punished?
Or even sent straight to hell for disobeying God without a second chance?
I'm glad God did what he did
Many never have the opportunity to do what Jesus did
Most of us probably wouldn't have the courage to commit such actions Jesus made
In spite of it all
We have a choice
Obey God's word and love him wholeheartedly or be a worker of iniquity
Time is running out
Make a decision
And be wise
Because although God is father and loving to all of his children
He loves us enough
To let us go
Choose WISELY

My Truth The Birthing

FIGHT

Angels surround us daily to war on our behalf.
Utilization must be at an all-time high.

TRIUMPH

Beyond the looks of this world
Only spiritual eyes can see
His glory
That raises me above the pillars of judgment
Into his heavenly light
I am ROYAL
I always win

My Truth The Birthing

FOOT MOVEMENT

Relaxing
Every area of my being
Waiting to unite with the one
Fingertips extended
Toes well equipped to move
Sounds of breaking
Shadows behind
Path clear
Faith
Uplifted
Aircraft off cruise control
Heart skipped on replay
Eyes zoomed
Feet
A breeze
Life
Lifted
Sound
Enlarged
Trail
Marked
Arise
Sound effect
Marker
Recorded
The future is clear and cold
I keep moving

Zoom
Zoom
Zoo.

Unstoppable
Destination at a distance
I keep moving

Dust settles
Green becomes brown
Yellow
To red
Blue
To grey

Full
To empty
Sun to clouds
Vision
Clear

I keep moving
I keep moving
I keep moving
I keep oo…

My Truth The Birthing

RAIN

Ashes arise out of the old
Rain pours into the new being
Spirit to spirit
Deep calls
Breath and new life appear
And are made new
A new man lives inside

HE WINS, I WIN

Period.

My Truth The Birthing

A NEW WOMAN

See something different?
I know you do
Can't figure it out
Can you?
See what you normally see is an insecure little girl
But know
When you see me
You are looking at a woman
A woman who is not afraid to speak her mind
People have tried to test me to see if I'm weak
But honey don't test me
Because as you can see I am not weak or helpless
Many years my life were so crazy
If anyone else walked in my shoes
They would have given up by now
But now
I can move on and continue the journey of becoming a woman
A woman who is smart, intelligent, and strong
Strong enough not to take the wrong things from anyone
A woman who is ready for life and its trials
I'm just
A new woman

TRUE INNER BEAUTY

My beauty is not my signature of my personality
My humbleness is
It's funny how life causes people to look from the outside in
When really
Your appearance doesn't define who you are
Don't get it twisted
Your actions can speak louder than words
But when it comes down to understanding where I am in this world
It's hard to click a button
Stop time
And pull the lever that's supposed to define me
See my inner conscious tells me this will never be known from a five minute conversation
Or a five second stare down
There is much more to me
How would you know if you've never taken out the time to visualize my true personality?
And well
Just me period
I'm not the average woman stuck on materialistic wants you see in the media
Or some double minded, self-arrogant or cocky individual looking for a handout
I'm just me
A young woman loving God
See
I may be a soldier but know

My Truth The Birthing

God has built me to be the woman I am today
It hasn't always been beautiful white clouds or a shining son
Believe me when I tell you
There have been times I've asked God why
But when I got down on my knees
One day at a time it took for me to gain my strength
I know those days
Where you feel like God isn't there
And you feel
Why should he forgive me?
Truth is
He never left and has always listened
That's how I know through it all
He's humbled me and with that comes an inner courage
Including misjudgments made by those
Who will never understand
My true inner beauty

A BEAUTIFUL FLOWER

Arise
As the sun rises into the clouds
With the birds and nature awakens
Can you hear them?
The whispering winds
The peace God brings day to day
Imagine
A seed in the ground
Waiting to burst
Into freedom
To blow within the weeds and the grass and the dirt
From day to day
They are watered and groomed gently
Just as a baby
So that it can grow and become a beautiful flower
Like me
It must learn its value
Understanding what it must become in life
Once it grows
The stem connects to the roots
Holding it all together
After while
The flower bursts into full bloom and is able to stand on its own and live
With nature
As God and the precious sun smiles down
It is beautiful

My Truth The Birthing

HARVEST

Open your eyes dear one
See what is before you
A field of freshly grown wheat, grass, and honey
And there is more
You are near
But you must walk to obtain the fullness there of

GLOVES HANDED OVER

I give up. I can't do it alone.

My Truth The Birthing

A DEEPER WOUND

Wrinkled skin
Smooth as a breeze
Smile as high as the summer in the brink of the morning hour
Her hair
Gray like the clouds in foreign countries
Fingers
Long enough to grab a hand and love with affection
Eyes
Truth revealed through one look turned in my direction

That was big mama

Laying in a bed
In her nineties
High spirit
Moving as strong as she could
While still needing assistance
Bold
Like a lion
Strength
As strong as the winds blowing throughout the rivers
She arose with great impact
These are the memories I have of her
Looking upon family videos
Reminiscing during parts of family reunions and scenes of her celebrations

This is what I have left
To remember the same trailblazer that kept our family strong
Imagining what it was like to just be like her

Arms folded
Dressed to the T
Summer hats
White gloves
Glasses
And yes
Food cooked to match her personality
Mmm..mmm.mmm…
The memories are vague
Slow to speed
Short to remember

The day her spirit arose
My mother got the call
And that morning she cried and called on Jesus
Over and over and over again
That was the moment
I knew my memories of her would fade

I remember
The day my mother gave me items to remember her
Perfume
Belt
Bracelet

It belonged to her

My Truth The Birthing

Big mama

Pieces of a woman I barely remember

A DIFFERENT WOUND

I remember the day it hit me
Memories I tried to hide and kept inside
Moments that I said to myself I would never speak of again
No one will ever find out
In that moment I cried and cried and cried
Even at the age of twenty six years old it still haunted me
My heart began to ache
Not even mommy and daddy understood my pain
Years and years I became bitter and angry
Repeatedly it ran through my mind daily
Hidden emotions I didn't know still lived there
I remember laying in the bed
Crying myself to sleep and saying that it would be ok
Wiped my face because no one needed or wanted to hear me in the night
I remember sitting in a chair writing poems
Beginning books about things that are rooted in our communities
Stories that go back to my African heritage that was still there
Things that no one else understood
Stories, chapters, and beginning books that I could never complete because I still had this pain in my memories that held me hostage
It prevented me from living out my destiny
Bitterness, anger, rage, insecurity, low self-esteem and pain
Head held down and feet barely moving

My Truth The Birthing

Weight increased, lies heard and believed
I began to believe the lies they said about me because they didn't understand my pain
They didn't understand the darkness, anger, and silence that came from memories of events from my past
They didn't understand in the midst of the worry and silence there was a hunger for more
To live
To have joy
To be comforted by something or someone that I didn't know already
Something that wasn't an easy fix
Something that could take the pain away because every day in my mind it thought this is it
Then he spoke to me and came into my life freely
Led me to the way of redemption
Something I never knew
Counseling helped
I must admit
I allowed myself to be fearful and stay in a place of being a victim and in bondage of living in the past I would stay where I couldn't move
An awakening had to come
So that I could finally
Spread my wings

MOTHERHOOD

Being a mother is something I always thought I would experience
I'm almost thirty years old and sometimes I feel defeated and disappointed because things didn't work out the way I wanted them to
I know God has a plan for my life
One of the greatest things that I can do is leave a great legacy for my children
So they would be able to know and tap into their purpose and destiny effortlessly and not let this world define them or their abilities
They would know that they are treasures and gifts to this world and never let it bypass them
I know who I am and I look at the promises or God for my life
To this day
I still find it difficult to not be a mother
The one thing God reminds me daily is I don't have to have natural children to be a mother
I can pour into children and remind them not to let this world define them or their abilities
They would know that they are treasures and never let this world pass them by
I know who I am and I look at the promises of God in my life to this day I still find it difficult to not be a mother
The one thing that God reminds me daily is I don't have to have natural children
That will follow in my footsteps

My Truth The Birthing

They will understand that this life I live is for them and those that will connect with my children as well That will be the beginning of a great legacy

"To my future children, I pray that you will never experience what I did. I pray you will have dreams that will never be measured by this world. Never get discouraged because of the naysayers. I pray that you will one day be mothers and fathers to those that need you the most. I pray you hold on to hope and remember you are built with destiny on the inside of you. Have hope and live life abundantly and rejoice in all things no matter what happens God is there with you, You have victory no matter what arises. I pray you know how much I love you and how much I fight every day so you have an opportunity to live. I pray you know that every sacrifice I made was for you and the legacy I leave behind. I pray that you tap into your purpose and identity and never let people decide who you are especially outside of food that says that you are. I pray you love and love hard. Never forget who you are."

Love,
Mom

SURRENDER

A real yes to God requires surrendering all of your ideas, plans, and your own will that you created for yourself.

My Truth The Birthing

MY LOVE FOR HIM

Sweet melodies of memories I never imagined
Until I met you
Beauty
Smiles of passion
The kind of love I never felt before
You gave me
You made me feel like it was us against the world
Why settle for something less than my standards when you found me?
A Queen
That's what you called me
Never letting judgmental tongues take precedence
Many times they tried to say we were dreaming
I thought dreams weren't illegal after all
That's what got us here in the first place
T always starts that way
We dreamed of how far we'll go in life
It's just a question of will we pursue it
We blend together like we're made for each other
I would never choose to leave you and I can't live without you
Every time I hear your voice I feel safe and at peace
I'm glad you came around
You seem to know a side of me no one else has been able to reach
My heart loves everything about you
Your style, words and emotions
You will always be my first love and forever be with me

LOVE LETTER

I've been waiting my whole life
To experience a love that's never ending
Just as Adam found Eve and gave her a part of him
It reminds me of God's love for us
He loves us so much that we may one day meet again to
share a lifetime of possibilities
To behold one another
Breathe into each other's soul
To reach deep down and one day grab hold of our deepest
fears and replace them
With a lifetime of happiness, fulfillment, joy and bliss
Our perfect satisfaction of each other can never be ruined
By temporary inconveniences
It's unlimited
You possess all that I am willing to give to you and more
My love for you goes past all of the flaws and irritations
caused by the affections of your beauty
Within
I know once we walk down the path of husband and wife
I will walk down the aisle
I will forever be tied to you
As my husband we will be united and blessed by God
And his angels that will look down on us and smile
And say
I bless this union

My Truth The Birthing

STRENGTH

Sometimes the strength you think you already obtain can keep you in a place of bondage if that strength doesn't come from God the father.
Don't fight on your own.

LITTLE BLACK GIRL

Little black girl
Why do you hang your head as low as the dirt upon the ground?
A place that you will never know
Because you are beautiful and intelligent
Little black girl
What do you dream?
How has life shown you truth and opportunity?
You are hope
Little black girl
Has your mother or father ever told you that you are special?
The winds and rain can't move fast enough
To obtain your knowledge and wisdom
Little black girl
You are important
God created you in his image and with purpose
Therefore you are a king
And just like Esther you were created for such a time as this
Little black girl
Pick up your feet
You are not a slave
You are a ruler
Lift up your eyes and see your land
Little black girl
You are great
Those that went before you

My Truth The Birthing

Are a reminder that you can accomplish the impossible
Little black girl
Open your eyes
Your beauty cannot be defined
You were created beyond perfection and simplicity
You are powerful
Little black girl
You are not a statistic
Your anatomy is more precious than a compliment
Greater than a temporary emotion
Your life is extravagant
Little black girl
Do you understand the meaning of worship?
Your hands, feet, and entire being belong to the king of kings
Sweetie don't hold back
You were made for his glory
Little black girl
Celebrate your freedom
You are the beginning of an outbreak
Your generation is depending on you
For strength, wisdom, courage, and leadership
Little black girl
Raise your hands high
You are a change agent
Grab your staff, instruments, pen, paper and whatever you need
Walk forward

ENCOURAGEMENT

After conception
A baby begins to develop
Month by month
Day by day
Without eyes or understanding in the first trimester
The child begins to depend on the mother for its
necessities
Until one day
It's birthed and realizes
After time
It always had everything it needed
With patience
And trust

My Truth The Birthing

RIDE OR DIE

See normally
I would keep my mouth shut and let people go about their business
But when it comes to my God and saving souls
It pushes me towards an urgency
To get the word of God revealed the best way I know how
Throughout the word using my voice
It's personal
Experiences have taught me to never let a person tear me away from his truth
He sent me with a purpose
To live my life the way he expected me
I am his child
That means less of me and more of him
Fasting, praying, believing, not doubting and living and leading by example
No childish games acing like I don't hear him
I must do all that he requires of me
My all
Like saying he knows my heart isn't enough
All of the lying, cheating, lusting, gossiping, arrogance, killing, destroying, isolation in churches, idols and everything in my life that's not at his approval
It all has to end
See I'm a ride or die chick
I don't mind receiving the funny looks, rolling of eyes,

And bad looks and words from others
I don't mind because I'm giving his creation a reality check
For the right reasons
You can choose to follow God or stay on your own
I just want to make it to heaven
The city with all of his promises
It's all worth it
He loves us enough
That if we live right he'll accept us to be with him
After all that time
It will be a beautiful feeling
I can imagine at the end
There will be no worries
No reasons to cry
Just dwell in his safety
What could be better than that?
You decide
Just know that heaven and hell is real
God is looking for his people to represent him
It's all fun and games for so long
Until reality checks in and hits you hard
He said in his word every knee shall bow and every tongue will confess
You can think you have all of the time in the world
But at the end of the day your last time could be tomorrow if not today
So open up your eyes to what is in front of you and open your ears so you can hear his voice
Because whether you know it or not
He's call you

My Truth The Birthing

STRENGTH

God's banner over me is love
It stretches beyond the pain
Stronger than my tears
Hope develops
In the middle of adversity
His love pushes me past envy
I am strong
I am lifted into his arms
And strengthened

GROWTH

As branches grow
The inner and outer textures may become thick
And firmly stretched
But it never detaches from the root
Soon
Through the season
Leaves are birthed and sprout boldly
Amongst the limbs
Freely

My Truth The Birthing

CHANGE

A long time ago
I was once told to never let a man define who I am
I didn't hear never let your trails, tests and enemies determine my future

Many times we let people and situations define who we are
I was blessed with greatness and certainty
That I will prosper and never give up
I've been through too much to let a little hit from the devil knock me down
Even when I thought about suicide
I felt there was nothing left
Then God reminded me that he created me with a clean heart
I remain humble and continue to be discerning and sensitive to his spirit
Never again will I remain in a negative state of mind
Thinking I can't make it and not having a desire to live my life
Never again will I question the greatness of my wonderful father
I shall prosper
I will prosper
I must prosper
You can't put this blessed woman down
And expect me not to get back up
There's no stopping me
The enemy should have never messed with me

I will forever be a fighter

My Truth The Birthing

WED

I always thought that I would be the one married
By the age of twenty-five
With memories full of love, compassion and grace
Upon my husband and my children and myself
Well it didn't work that way
I look at my past
My present
My future
I wonder
Was it something I did?
Was it something I missed?
Or is it just it may never happen in my lifetime?
I want to be the one to represent true kingdom love
demonstration and healthy marriage some days it
feels like it won't happen for me
It is hard to admit because I know
Even at the age of twenty-eight
God has a divine purpose, timing and knows all that
will happen in my life right now
It is hard to see it
I've done so much in my life
I've experienced so much and it still feels like I'm
behind and it'll never happen
Or I have to wait years and years
I remember telling God a long time ago
No matter how long it takes I will wait and give him
my yes
I won't move ahead of him because I know what

those that went before me had to overcome
I refuse to repeat cycles
Even in the way I feel burdens
A lack of patience
Like I'm on the time clock
Because I want to have two children and adopt two children
There were men that came in my life
I thought they were the one
I spent eight years of my life in the past thinking I was living my life to the fullest
Really
It was because of my own lack of knowledge and understanding the life that he has given me
In the choices I made for myself

Now I'm preparing and waiting
Living the life I believe God wants me to have and making decisions daily
I know
One day a potential interest will come in my lifetime
There will be a great harvest and fruitfulness will come
My children won't repeat the cycles of those that went before then
We will raise and teach them that they too can focus on the things of the Lord and live their life to the fullest that God has for them

My Truth The Birthing

MOVING ON

I choose to no longer blame others for my progress in life. I have a responsibility and my time is now to be free.

THE JOURNEY CONTINUES

God leads
I will follow him forever

The Journey Continues

www.ingramcontent.com/pod-product-compliance
Lightning Source LLC
LaVergne TN
LVHW021623080426
835510LV00019B/2728